Hidden by Gender

What Women Need to Know About Gender Bias to Shine
in the Corporate Space & the Marketplace

BETH HAND

www.leadershiphand.com

Dedication

To those who broke ground and are breaking ground…
For an inclusive world where everyone can shine.

Table of Contents

Hidden By Gender

What Women Need to Know About Gender Bias to
Shine in the Corporate Space & the Marketplace

Welcome Bold and Brilliant Readers

"Countries with higher levels of gender equality have higher economic growth. Companies with more women on their boards have higher returns. Peace agreements that include women are more successful. Parliaments with more women take up a wider range of issues - including health, education, anti-discrimination, and child support."

—Ban Ki-moon
United Nations Secretary-General
International Women's Day, 2014

Welcome, bold, brilliant women.

I wrote this book for you—smart women who want to make a contribution and have a bigger impact on the world. As a woman leader, you have such power and strength.

When I say make a contribution and have a bigger impact—these are however *you* uniquely define them given *your* unique business circumstances.[1], whether you are leading your own company in the marketplace or leading within a company in the corporate space.

For some of you, it's the thrill and challenge of becoming a trusted brand with raving fans. For others, it's ensuring that the values and culture you founded the business on are alive and well as your company grows and changes. Maybe it's contributing to long-term economic growth in an emerging economy like the high-impact entrepreneurs Endeavor.[2], led by Chief Executive Officer (CEO) and co-founder Linda Rottenberg, work with.

If you are in the corporate space, you may define contribution and impact by taking on a bigger leadership role within the company or setting your sites on the C-Suite, the CEO or other top executive position. Maybe it's championing an initiative that's good business for the company and the world.

The purpose of this book is to help you be at your best while making your contribution and to help you show up every day shining in all your brilliance and helping others show up in theirs.

∞

When I met my first coach, Teri-E Belf[3], long before coaching was mainstream, it was pivotal: I understood immediately how coaching could help develop my leadership skills and, in turn, achieve better business results. What I didn't know then was that the very things I needed to succeed in an organization were the same things I would need to succeed as a business owner. Even with my increasing competency, I also came to understand the importance of the bigger context into which women are born, live, and lead in the world. **It's this perspective—seeing the playing field and learning to navigate it—that is the foundation for this book.**

This isn't meant to be a definitive work written by an expert in gender research. I'll leave that in the capable hands (and minds) of people like Mayra Buvinić, Senior Fellow, United Nations (UN) Foundation. She is the lead author of the UN Foundation and ExxonMobil Foundation's *A Roadmap for Promoting Women's Economic Empowerment*[4]. Rather, it is meant to share my expertise in leadership development from almost two decades working with leaders in Fortune 500, small and mid-size companies, and mission-driven interests worldwide. It is also meant to share what I've learned as a woman and as a woman business owner to help you shine at your brightest in the corporate space and the marketplace.

I'm writing to women in countries with the political stability and economic infrastructure to focus on leading a company or business. You may be leading in a Fortune 500 company, leading a **Small and Medium Enterprise (SME)**, or a **Small and Growing Business (SGB)** as defined by the Aspen Network of Development Entrepreneurs.[5] (ANDE). ANDE's definition of an SGB is:

"Commercially viable businesses with five to 250 employees that have significant potential, and ambition, for growth. Typically, SGBs seek growth capital from $20,000 to $2 million."

To help you and those you lead, this book is divided into three parts:

Part 1. Seeing the big picture and understanding the global context into which we are born, live, and lead.

Part 2. Discovering where gender is a red herring that hides women and men, revealing the playing field, and adopting a practical mindset to help level it.

Part 3. Practical, powerful high-level strategies to help you shine in the corporate space and the marketplace.

Finally, for those women and men who broke ground for me and other women, I offer a deep bow of gratitude and a heartfelt thank you.

Now, let's get going!

PART 1

Understanding the Larger Context: How Women Are Hidden Around the World

Malala and Microsoft's CEO:
A Snapshot of Women's and Girls' Rights

One morning, I woke to the news that Malala Yousafzai had won the Nobel Peace Prize at age 17. As a young Pakistani girl, Malala had been speaking out for girls' education. The Taliban issued a death threat and attempted to assassinate her on a school bus. She survived. She came to international attention for her humble heroism and as an advocate for children's education and in particular, girls' education.

Five minutes later, I was watching a television clip of Microsoft's CEO Satya Nadella saying women shouldn't ask for raises, but trust karma. In the clip, you could practically hear the deadly silence of collective disbelief in the auditorium at such bad advice—silence that filled my living room as well.

From developing to developed countries, women and girls are denied equality. We can't just "trust karma," and this isn't just a story of male dominance—it's more complex than that. But, when we don't see the inequality, or work to promote equal rights, it hurts us all—men, women, boys, and girls.

The International Finance Corporation[6] is working to eliminate gender barriers in the private sector. It reports that women:

"have less access to equal employment opportunities and capital to grow their businesses, experience high levels of sexual

violence, are often barred from owning or inheriting land or other property, and have less income to invest for the future."

The difference between women in the United States (U.S.), where I live, and developing countries is an order of magnitude: my survival isn't at stake, I have rights and know about them, and I can own property. But, when it comes to business and work, I see the overlap between overt and covert bias that keeps our light from shining as brightly as possible.

To provide perspective on just how recently women in America have been afforded the rights we do have, consider that, had I founded my company in 1987, I would not have been able to get business credit in my name. I would have had to go to my father, brother, or uncle to co-sign. Yes, you read that correctly. As recently as 1987, before the passage of the Women's Business Ownership Act in 1988, women could not procure business credit without the assistance of a man. In the United States, women's right to vote is only two years older than my 92-year-old mother! There is a lot to appreciate in our country, though in some practices calling ourselves a developed country seems a misnomer. Legally, the playing field for women in the U.S. is more level than in the recent past, but globally, women are still struggling to overcome the cultural norms that dictate the rights and behaviors of women.

As a career woman, and later when I founded Leadership Hand, I thought the world would be my oyster. I couldn't see that my family culture and the national culture hid me and other women. In some ways, I was hidden from myself. I assumed the difficulties I couldn't quite name were leadership competencies I lacked. It has taken me a while to see that the playing field was not level, and I'm still learning how to master the game.

When I heard Nadella's words, I didn't hear him speak as a person, or even an industry leader. His was the voice of a global issue that isn't relegated to a distant school in Pakistan. **We have to acknowledge that gender inequalities, both obvious and hidden, occur in all cultures, in developed and developing countries.**

Women, you see the cultural gender blind spots you're up against. The overt ones, and the covert ones. The double standard women continue to face affects our level of influence, our positions of power, and our financial interests. Even *Time Magazine* added the word "feminism" to its 2014 list of words to be banned, with the explanation it had "become a thing that every celebrity had to state their position on whether this word applies to them, like some politician declaring a party…." *Time's* article was swiftly followed by public backlash and a retraction. Roxane Gay wrote in *The Washington Post:*

"I keep trying to imagine a universe in which too many public figures declaring themselves feminists would be a bad thing. This would have to be a universe where 'the issues,' as the poll vaguely mentions, no longer exist—one where women enjoy unlegislated reproductive freedom and have easy, affordable access to birth control."

Many of you are actively engaged in human rights, gender, and inclusiveness issues on a global scale. Even if you aren't working at this level, you can do something to strengthen and support those with less power right where you are. The solution has to be both an acknowledgement of reality and an action to ensure parity. This is the only way we'll change our culture to be more inclusive and to contribute to a thriving economic and social ecosystem. It's important for all humans.

Wherever you are, be your most brilliant business and leadership self so you can shine in the world and the marketplace. It's a case of "act locally; impact globally." And bring others along. You are the rising tide, and it's the rising tide that lifts (and rights) all boats.

Life or Death for Women and Girls

The reality is that it's an unequal world you and I were born into. Be aware of it—deeply aware, and stand up on behalf of yourself and others: women and men, girls and boys.

You know and see the physical differences between men and women, boys and girls. You see the biological differences between men and women. But, nature is not what hides women. **What hides women is the cultural and social context into which they are conceived and born.** Cultural and social context determines who lives or dies, who is fed, who is educated, who has rights. It determines who is seen or hidden by virtue of his or her gender. For so many women and girls, the lack of human rights invokes both heartbreak and outrage.

How girls and women are treated varies by country, region, and household. In some cultures, female fetuses are aborted, or if a second girl is born into a family, she is killed. When I think my challenges are hard, I remember that I am *alive*. My culture and my family said I counted.

In conflict regions, rape is a tool of war meant to demoralize and undermine the men and women of societies or groups upon whom it is wrought. In some cultures, traditions supported by both men and women have consequences for girls and their futures. For example, the ritual cutting of a girl's genitalia causes a lifetime of pain and infection, or the tradition of child marriages precludes a girl's chance to an education. In other countries, it might mean women do not have the right to vote, to own property, or to own a business.

If women do have those rights, the challenges become issues like access to credit and financial instruments (like a bank account instead of a hole dug in the ground), and access to markets, training, and business networks. These are the same challenges women businesses confront in the U.S.

As I said earlier, the issues aren't relegated to a distant school in Pakistan. We've come a long way and still have a long way to go.

Many public and private organizations are making a difference. Whole generations in developed countries are growing up aware of the bigger world with a sense of responsibility to helping others. The media is playing its part covering stories around the world. Technology is enabling voices to be heard and injustices to be witnessed by all. It is enabling access to financial instruments, market information, and training. All play their part.

My money is on women leaders and business owners as the great equalizers, harmonizers, and catalysts for global good. It's an excellent bet.

The Top and Bottom Countries for Women

One annual report, the *Global Gender Gap Report*[7], from the World Economic Forum takes on the daunting task of quantifying the impact of gender gaps in four key areas:

- Economic Participation and Opportunity
- Educational Attainment
- Health and Survival
- Political Empowerment

Let's take a look at the top and bottom 20 percent of 142 countries for women in 2014.

World Economic Forum
The Global Gender Gap Report 2014

Top 20% for Women		Bottom 20% for Women	
Rank	Country	Rank	Country
1	Iceland	115	United Arab Emirates
2	Finland	116	Qatar
3	Norway	117	Korea, Repu.
4	Denmark	118	Nigeria
5	Sweden	119	Zambia
6	Nicaragua	120	Bhutan
7	Rwanda	121	Angola
8	Ireland	122	Fiji
9	Philippines	123	Tunisia
10	Belgium	124	Bahrain
11	Switzerland	125	Turkey
12	Germany	126	Algeria
13	New Zealand	127	Ethiopia
14	Netherlands	128	Oman
15	Latvia	129	Egypt
16	France	130	Saudi Arabia
17	Burundi	131	Mauritania
18	South Africa	132	Guinea
19	Canada	133	Morocco
20	United States	134	Jordan
21	Ecuador	135	Lebanon
22	Bulgaria	136	Côte d'Ivoire
23	Slovenia	137	Iran, Islamic Rep.
24	Australia	138	Mali
25	Moldova	139	Syria
26	United Kingdom	140	Chad
27	Mozambique	141	Pakistan
28	Luxembourg	142	Yemen

Legal Rights:
An Indicator Whether Women Are Seen

You know that women are acknowledged when:

- There are laws that confer equal rights.
- People (women and men) know about these laws.
- Laws are enforced.

All three must be in place. Even if all three are in place, and thus, in theory, have a measure of equality, the reality can be quite different.

The Johns Hopkins School of Advanced International Studies convened a panel on women as change agents in post-conflict societies. One panelist commented that although Nicaragua had been ranked as having the greatest improvement in gender equality, when she asked Nicaraguan women about this ranking, they shook their heads. They agreed there was progress that showed up in the form of policy, but in practice, the reality was *not* one of equality.

For those women with rights to own property, to vote or own a business, gender inequalities are clear when other women don't have these. But, a culture of freedom and rights is still new. When you forget this as a woman in a developed or less developed country, you are forgetting the larger context into which you were born or are now living. You may be subject to the undertow of bias. Being aware of it can help you make faster, more powerful headway to the shore.

Some Recent History of
Women's Rights and New Precedence

In 1975, the first world conference on women, the International Women's Year, was held in Mexico City. The Second World Conference on Women was held in Copenhagen in 1980. The third in Nairobi, in 1985, and the fourth conference, the Fourth World Conference on Women was held in Beijing, 1995. All of these conferences broke new ground focusing on women contributing to the powerful momentum and emphasis on women today. We have so much to lean on: experience, strength, and hope for women and girls everywhere.

However, no matter how much progress there is, changes and improvements can begin to backslide. Deborah Rubin is co-founder of Cultural Practice LLC, a women-owned business, and has a Ph.D. in Anthropology. At a Society for International Development[8] Gender and Inclusive Development event, she reminded participants that you have to keep working at inclusion and equal rights.[9].

For people and organizations focused on the rights of women and girls, the Fourth World Conference on Women is like the Big Bang. For example, it gave birth to the U.S. government's Vital Voices Democracy Initiative. It was established in 1997 by then-First Lady Hillary Rodham Clinton and former Secretary of State Madeleine Albright. Since then, it became a nongovernmental organization, the Vital Voices Global Partnership.[10]. Vital Voices is advancing women's economic, political, and social status around the world. It has trained and mentored 14,000 women in over 144 countries. President and CEO Alyse Nelson and her organization live the mission of ensuring women have a seat at the table and in life.

At the annual Vital Voices Global Leadership Awards event in 2015, former U.S. President Bill Clinton said that while "the headlines are discouraging, the trend line is good [for women and the world]." "You," he reminded all of us, "are that trend line."

Nationally, Public Broadcasting Service (PBS) in the United States has created an extraordinary documentary series called *Makers: Women Who Make America*[11]. Each documentary showcases women who have changed American institutions: in business, in politics, in space, in Hollywood, in comedy, and in war. It focuses on what they have confronted and what they have overcome. Watching, I've laughed at the absurdities, cried at the indignities and cheered the victories. While the stories are U.S. focused, the inspiration transcends nationality.

When we can see the fight that's been fought, and know that you and I are reaping the benefits, we can lean back on the women who've gone before us for strength. Strengthened, we can take our place right here, right now.

Here are a few examples of recent changes in women's rights, both formal and informal:

- In the U.S., H.R. 5050, formerly called "The Women's Business Ownership Act of 1988," entitled women business owners to get credit for their businesses without having a male relative sign. It established the National Women's Business Council[12] to report annually to Congress and the President on barriers to success for women

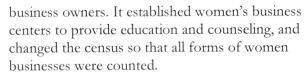

business owners. It established women's business centers to provide education and counseling, and changed the census so that all forms of women businesses were counted.

- At a Women's Foreign Policy Group[13] celebration of women diplomats, one diplomat after another said they were the first female to hold the post. They appreciated their roles and equally looked forward to a time when that distinction of "first female to…" was no longer part of anyone's introduction. In other words, when a female diplomat is no longer called out as being the first female, she's simply a diplomat.
- In Switzerland, women received the right to vote[14] in 1971.
- As of 2015, women hold only 4.6 percent of CEO positions in Standard & Poor's 500 companies[15] as reported by Catalyst, a nonprofit organization that promotes inclusive workplaces for women.

Elizabeth Vazquez & WEConnect International
Helps Women Businesses Globally
Be Seen in the Marketplace

"Women make up half the population, so [we] aren't a minority, but when it comes to doing business, we are." "Women," says Vazquez, "are just invisible."

When Elizabeth Vazquez[16] talks about women as an emerging market, her eyes sparkle, and she speaks with energetic optimism. She is the President, CEO and co-founder of WEConnect International[17]. Vazquez knows how hard it is for women in developing countries and transition economies—countries transitioning to free markets, where markets determine prices—to be a part of the global value chain. A value chain is the entire range of activities by people and businesses to bring a product or service to consumers: from the coffee bean farm to your grocery store shelves, and everyone in between.

Vazquez's and WEConnect's vision is to help women businesses be valued in the marketplace. They want women to have access to the right knowledge and networks to get into corporate and large government value chains where the money is really being spent. This has the potential for massive impact in our lifetime—trillions of dollars in implications. It's not just because the women are going to be benefiting directly, but because of

17

how women spend their money. They spend it on their families and their communities. Her book, co-authored with Andrew Sherman, *Buying for Impact: How to Buy from Women and Change Our World*, makes the compelling business case for getting women-owned businesses into global supply chains.

Her story is important for three reasons:

1. It addresses a global problem women-run businesses face—access to markets.

2. It is an example of bold and brilliant leadership—knowing when to change the business model and having the courage to do so to bring the vision to life.

3. It illustrates how a business model must adjust for different markets in different regions around the globe.

The Starting Point:
A Certification Organization

The starting point was WEConnect International, based on the U.S. model of the Women's Business Enterprise National Council[18] (WBENC), an organization that certifies businesses as woman-owned. WBENC has a very strict definition of what a certified woman-owned business is. The vision of the corporate members was to find women-owned businesses globally and certify that they were women-owned businesses. In short, WEConnect was primarily a certification organization.

With a very sophisticated economy like in the U.S., having strict standards makes sense. The U.S. has a history of certification standards and thousands of existing certified women-owned businesses that are well organized. Outside the U.S.? That just isn't the case.

An Issue of Inclusion:
Seeing Women All Over the World

Vazquez knew they had to build a pipeline to women businesses, so larger businesses could find suppliers and service providers. Focusing on certification only wasn't going to get the job done. WEConnect needed to make a fundamental shift—from a certification organization to an education organization. This would change how WEConnect thought of itself, how other people understood it and its ability to go to market.

Vazquez considered it an issue of inclusion.

"We have women all over the world that meet our criteria, in every country that should be contributing to this network and benefiting from it. But, unless we chose to be inclusive and flexible, and offer a way for them to get involved that didn't require a strict certification, we weren't going to be able to achieve global impact."

WEConnect had the support from countries, corporate executives, government executives, and association leaders, all wanting to promote the model of WEConnect and be part of this network they were hearing about. What WEConnect didn't have was the infrastructure to offer certification with trained assessors in all those countries, nor would they have it any time soon. For a lot of women who did meet the organization's strict standards and criteria, even if they wanted to get certified, the cost and reality of no assessors was going to prevent it.

Women as an Emerging Market: Changing Minds to Reach the Invisible

Vazquez showed an extraordinary wisdom and resiliency. As she went to market, she observed and responded to what was happening. The original model wasn't going to work, and the objective needed to shift. The very things she'd initially advocated for—a certification organization, she now had to back track on. She went back to the corporate members, potential members, and partner organizations that had paved the way in the United States, as well as those that WEConnect had educated outside of the U.S.

She had to paint the biggest picture of all—women as an emerging market, and how to help women businesses in every part of the world.

In six months, lightning speed really, Vazquez was able to argue that certification couldn't be the starting point. They needed to adjust for different markets and to do so by offering self-registration to reach women business owners.

"We really literally just had to sit and listen [to the corporate members and partner organizations]. We had to explain to them what we wanted to do and why. And then we had to listen to what their concerns were, what were the fears, what were the objections, what were their perceptions of the alternative options to what we were proposing."

Fully Seeing Those We Want to Help

What Vazquez and her team did was fully see women businesses around the world, and what would help them have access to global markets. They recognized that looking through the lens of the U.S. experience meant seeing women in the strongest, most powerful countries and overlooking those with a huge percentage of the poorest of the poor. WEConnect kept the requirement that a woman had to own 51 percent of the business, for example. For self-registration, women businesses still have to meet certification criteria. WEConnect helped and continues to help women meet industry standards and educate them about the importance of ramping up their business game.

Fully Seeing the Objective

Vazquez says,

"When you look at trade, people think that it's kind of overwhelming and it's complicated and it's hard. But, at the end of the day, trade is just people, that's all; people building relationships. Do I trust that you're going to give me what I ask for, and are you going to pay me what you say you're going to pay me?"

You're going to hear more on the topic of trust and trade later on.

"To maximize opportunities for businesses that haven't been able to do business together historically, you have to make everything super easy," says Vazquez. *"Even though it's still hard, our job is to try to make it as easy as possible."* She adds, *"What would make it easier for business to be conducted, for connections to be made? That's really our role."* And that's just what her organization is continuing to do today.

Blind Spots & Double Standards
that Hide Women

Ask any female leader and she can tell you about rules. More frequently, she can tell you about implicit rules—where there is one standard for men and another for women. How directly or indirectly you experience it, how strong or weak, and how many layers it is filtered through can vary wildly based on culture—a country's or a region's, an industry's, or an organization's.

That double standard isn't just one that men hold women to; women can hold other women to it as well. While I *know* bias exists, sometimes it's hard to prove definitively where women *seem* to have equal rights.

When Women and Men Are Blind to Discrimination

When your economic opportunities are tied to those with the most power, you may choose not to speak up when you experience bias—intentional or unintentional. I know I have. The most powerful person in a business alliance began weekly meetings with a joke about "a dumb woman" or sex, sometimes both. I didn't say anything even as I cringed. I didn't want to jeopardize the business relationship and knew that, for him, speaking up would be perceived as disloyalty, which he abhorred. When people laughed at his jokes, I wondered whether it was funny to them or if it was self-preservation.

A male CEO told me, "I don't believe women are treated unequally, and they certainly aren't here." He is the CEO. His role has the most power and authority in the company, second only to the board of directors. His view is a common one that people with power hold.

People, whether male or female, and groups that have power can be blind to what it is like for those with less power.

I was at a women's gathering featuring women from "both sides of the aisle." The phrase refers to the U.S. Congress where the two main political parties for the Senate and the House sit on either side of a wide aisle. The youngest member on the dais, a student who had been elected to head a student political party at her university, said gender bias didn't exist in her election and had not been an issue for her. The room seemed to take in a deep breath—there was an instant where no glasses clinked and background sounds stopped. The moderator moved on to ask about the experiences of the other women on the dais. All currently held or had recently held political office. All agreed they had experienced moderate to significant bias. Further, all agreed that they'd experienced more of it from older, white men in one party than in another party.

Surprising Research:
Women Who Experience Bias Deny It

In the case of this emerging political leader, it could be that in the university context, gender wasn't an issue. But, there is surprising and disturbing research that leads to a different conclusion. In a much-quoted study cited in a *Harvard Business Review* article, Faye Crosby[19] found that:

"Most women are unaware of having personally been victims of gender discrimination and deny it even when it is objectively true and they see that women in general experience it."

In her research, Crosby found that women were most likely to answer "no" to the question, "Are you at present the victim of sex discrimination?" Those very same women answered, "yes," when asked, "Are women discriminated against?" Faye goes on to explain what's behind this:

1. Cognitive bias is a factor: we find it much easier to conclude discrimination is occurring when we have aggregate data (about a class of people or a group). We find it much harder to do so when it's an individual.

2. People experience discomfort confronting their own victimization and having to assume another group or individual actively caused them to suffer. They deny disadvantage because they need to believe in a just world.

If you don't see bias or recognize its influence on you or others—particularly those with less power, you have a blind spot that may hinder your ability to lead.

Industries Can Be Blind Too

The International Finance Corporation is making the business case for women's participation in the labor force and business ownership. They've emphasized the importance of inclusion in the financial sectors to increase women's access to capital and financial instruments like a savings account, and offer sound guidance for policy makers. Yet, one bank that claimed it was female-friendly, asked women who came in where their husbands were. This was not exactly female-friendly.

Organizations are like people: there are discrepancies between theory and practice, espoused theory—the world view and values people believe and say their actions are based on, and theories in use—and what their actual behavior implies.[20]. Second, as we've already seen, if you haven't experienced bias first hand, you may not believe it exists.

Organizational Bias Can Be Hard to Pin Down

An executive in a multi-billion dollar company engaged me to work with his "almost perfect C-level executive" to smooth out her rough edges. He had never directly experienced the "rough edges," but was hearing about them from others. In our initial meeting, she was incisive, direct, and forthcoming, all of which could easily be perceived as edges—none of which you'd want any executive to relinquish.

I wondered if the individual was being held to a double standard because of the language the executive used in his initial request "almost perfect" and "she needs her edges smoothed." I also wondered if it were because of the industry, which is traditionally male-dominated and hierarchical. My conversations with her, the results of a 360-degree assessment with input from peers, direct reports, senior management, and anecdotal information provided more data to support my hunch that she might be being held to a double standard.

The classic dilemma[21] for women leaders is whether to be respected or liked. When a woman *is* bold and outspoken, tough on people, etc., women and men can hold her to a double standard. Her behavior isn't likeable, and the message is that women must behave in a likeable manner. Sheryl Sandberg, Facebook's COO, points out,

> *"Women are perceived as too soft or too tough, but never just right, and as competent or likeable, but rarely both[22]."*

Organizational gender bias however, can be hard to pin down and even harder to prove. Ellen Pao filed a gender discrimination suit against her employer—Kleiner Perkins Caufield & Byers. The company is a Silicon Valley venture capital firm prominent in the tech industry. In spite of telltale signs of discrimination, she lost.

Powerful Women's Blind Spots and Behaviors That Can Get in the Way in the Corporate Space

Powerful women can have blind spots and behaviors that cause backlash or negative feedback that surprises them. When organizational gender bias is present as well (or present in a few key people), those behaviors become a dangerous, career-limiting game. When a woman business owner has these traits, people might not like it, but she is given more latitude due to her role as founder and her position of power than a leader in an organization is given.

As she rises in the organization or the organization evolves, a woman leader may be asked to temper or change attributes she's cultivated and been rewarded for in the past. Women can feel frustrated at the mixed signals.

Here are some common blind spots that lead to problem behaviors:

- **Technical or industry experts who really are the smartest ones in the room.** Intellectual intelligence does *not* equal leadership intelligence. As women rise in the organization (or there are changes within the organization), they begin getting feedback that their behavior needs to change. Frequently, they need to cultivate their communication skills and develop their leadership skills.

- **Women who don't recognize the one-two punch of their positional power and communication style.** You think you are giving reasoned, direct feedback to a subordinate. They interpret it as painful criticism. This can happen with subordinates who aren't as confident as you assume them to be, and whose communication style is not as direct as your own. They can hold a powerful woman leader to a double standard.

- **When a woman hasn't found her own leadership style.** Her behavior may be inconsistent with her values. For example, she might be modeling an assertive style when she is less assertive or conversely, trying to temper how naturally assertive she is. People sense the incongruence and respond negatively to it.

- **When a woman is under major stress outside work.** While I advocate for leader's work-life integration, some women attempt to compartmentalize work and home. Usually, that's with good reason. The situation could be highly personal, or it could make her vulnerable if she's in a highly competitive environment. But, major stress leaks. It can impact our behavior in ways we aren't even aware of. Others are, however, even without knowing the details. The first step is acknowledging just how much stress you are under. Then get support. Don't simply tough it out. You'll be surprised at the immense relief you'll feel if you have a trusted advisor, confidante, or a mental health professional to speak with.

Your Family's Influence: Seeing the Era of Your Ways...

In my family lineage, my mother's great, great grandfather gave 100 acres equally to his sons and daughters. I stand taller when I remember this fact.

My mother's mother, my grandmother, was the first certified nurse in her state. My mother began an investment club when a woman's role was that of housewife. She has laid brick, poured cement, and worked as an office manager. She was also raised in a culture and at a time when women were "proper." Matching suits and handbags, coiffed hair, and painted fingernails were the order of the day. She was very clear that certain behaviors were ladylike and others were not.

Selling dahlias—large, beautiful flowers—to neighbors from my little red Radio Flyer wagon wasn't ladylike. I had to return any money I'd made. It was an early lesson that promoting yourself wasn't ladylike. Fast forward to adulthood, and I repeatedly had trouble marketing my business or owning my expertise. My behavior wasn't just affected by the family influence, it was shaped by regional cultural norms for women and girls, too. I'm still learning, but I see the playing field more clearly now as well as how people—men and women, can allow old stories and beliefs to get in our way.

> Hetty Green was an American businesswoman who lived in the 1800s. In her time, Green's business savvy made her as wealthy as Warren Buffet and Bill Gates. She was called the "Witch of Wall Street" for her penuriousness and other traits. That might be true, but I wonder how much of that moniker had more to do with engaging in "male" business. Green, in my estimation, rocked.

Vindicated: When Hidden Bias Is Clearly Revealed

When you encounter those times of overt, shocking unfairness like gender bias or double standards (whether self-imposed or imposed by others), thank your lucky stars! You've just been given a moment of clarity. Let that be a springboard into action. It is the subtleties—the ones you sense but can't quite prove (or convince others of) that can erode your confidence.

We've discussed some of the reasons for bias:

- Cultural context.
- When women can be liked or respected, but not both.
- When those in power can't see what it is like for those who aren't.
- Women's own cognitive bias.

There are times when I can second-guess myself about whether I've really just experienced bias, and earlier in my career, I wondered if I was deluding myself.

Then I came across an article in *The Washington Post*[23] newspaper about neurobiologist Ben Barres, who changed his sex from a woman to a man. Barres confirms that he receives more respect as a man. He has heard such jaw-dropping comments as, "Ben Barres gave a great seminar today, but then his work is much better than his sister's." What?! The person commenting had no idea that the intellectual capacity of Ben Barres, the man, and his sister were one and the same. Barres had changed sexes. He is transgender.

I felt vindicated. Bias wasn't "all in my head."

There is a new generation maturing that considers women equal and where gender lines don't fall neatly into male or female, accompanied by an increasing awareness of gender fluidity. In her TEDxWomen talk, Fifty Shades of Gay[24], iO Tillett Wright talks about creating a photographic record of anyone who didn't consider themselves 100 percent straight. She asked people who were LGBTQ (lesbian, gay, bisexual, transgender, and questioning—someone who is questioning his or her sexuality) to assign a percentage to how straight or gay they were. Most were in gray areas. Fortunately, there are segments of society moving toward an inclusiveness that embraces everyone.

"Well I do think, when there are more women, that the tone of the conversation changes, and also the goals of the conversation change. But it doesn't mean that the whole world would be a lot better if it were totally run by women. If you think that, you've forgotten high school."

—Madeleine Albright
Former U.S. Secretary of State
First woman to hold this role

Transforming Anger

When I was earning a Master in Business Administration, all the courses required team projects. One stood out in a bad way, layered with gender bias. I could type. In middle school, the girls were sent to typing class. I don't even remember where the boys were sent— they just weren't with us. Fast forward to being a young professional in graduate school. As the only one who could type on the team, I was expected to type our lengthy report. That may not sound like such a big deal now, but I wasn't a great typist. When I tired and made repeated mistakes, I was expected to keep going regardless. I kept trying and then stopped. One man tried to type, pecking with two fingers, and gave up. I resented being relegated to what was a traditionally subordinate role (typist). My attitude made a bad situation worse.

As I progressed in my career, I found more reasons to be angry about gender bias. It looked like "a man's world" and that women were shut out of "the boys club." These were partial truths. It was also true that I needed to develop political savvy and my leadership skills. I had no mentor, no group to learn from, and no coach. Here's the trap with anger or resentment: negative emotions help us survive in the short-term, but it's the positive ones that help us survive in the long term.[25]. Anger is most useful when it becomes a force for productive action. Otherwise, it is a distraction and a waste of your precious life energy. Part of your power and light is hidden.

Men Are the Disposable Sex

In the late 1990s, a colleague recommended Warren Farrell's book, *The Myth of Male Power: Why Men Are the Disposable Sex.* (This work came before Farrell and his followers went in a radical direction). He looked across cultures around the globe. He made a well-researched case that male power is a myth and that men are the disposable gender. They are the ones we send out to the field and to war.

Men frequently experience depression that goes undiagnosed and suffer silently because they are acculturated not to talk about perceived weakness. A study of large companies shows that men often die within just a few years of retiring. The loss of identity and not communicating about emotions plays a deadly role for them.

I came to realize something: men in the workplace are people too. The bias and exclusion I had experienced, I in turn, had rained down on others. This realization contributed to what you are reading today. I wanted an equal world for all without defaulting to unproductive blame. Women and men are better served when women are gender diplomats—standing firmly for equal rights *and* making a place for men. This is when it's no longer "half the sky" but the whole sky.

Is It a "Woman Thing," a "Man Thing," or a Competency Anyone Can Learn?

I was engaged by the CEO of an international association to help his senior leadership team perform well year-round. Not just at key events for the association members.

The team wasn't aware of its own "special sauce"— where they were brilliant. (This is quite common in individual leaders as well as teams.) I also discovered that the CEO engaged in confrontation and heated discussion in team meetings. To the CEO, this was "healthy discussion." Several members took their cue from him and engaged in the same behaviors. Other members, male and female, refrained from sharing opinions to avoid verbal conflict. They didn't push back on ideas or share valuable information—both things the CEO valued and wanted.

Massachusetts Institute of Technology (MIT) conducted research[26] that found the collective intelligence of a group is determined by three things:

1. The average social perceptiveness of the group members.

2. The evenness of conversational participation.

3. The proportion of women in the group.

The conclusion? Women raise the collective intelligence of groups. Yes, I was secretly pleased when I read this, then skeptical. I've worked with women leaders in dire need of social perceptiveness. That perceptiveness is important for ensuring more evenness in conversations. This is a gender-neutral skill, and it can be learned by anyone—male or female.

I helped the team discover guidelines for when they excelled and showed them how to translate them into day-to-day behaviors. That was important. But maybe more so was working with the CEO and the team on their social perceptiveness and how to ensure evenness among all members during team discussions. I got a great letter from the CEO some time later. Their work paid off in the team's performance year-round.

Men Are on the Gender Journey Too

Men can still be hidden today, and their views can still hide women. The older generations may not understand "what all the fuss is about" with women. I mean, after all, women can drive cars and have careers, can't they? Isn't that equality... what more could women want? There are younger generations too that overlook women or don't accord them equal rights. Don't write people with these views off—bring them along. They are products of culture, and they too are trying to find their way in a changing world.

When I was in Turkey consulting for the General Directorate of Revenues on a country-wide project crucial to its financial restructuring, I encountered what I perceived as gender bias. Not from my Turkish colleagues—from my American counterpart. The message I got from him was that my path as a female, a professional with a career, was the inferior one: his wife did not work. I didn't know if that's the message he had intended. Had I been a gender diplomat and inquired into his views, it would have been a chance to share mine and been enlightening for us both.

A U.S. diplomat worked in a country office where the culture was highly discriminatory against women. Over time, the American men, influenced by the country and office culture they were in, began to treat the American women this way. Culture, to use Geert Hofstede's definition, "is the collective programming of the mind that distinguishes one group from another." It began programming the men without the men even knowing it, although the women certainly did.

You have choices. You can educate and inform people. When you are in a position of power, you can insist they engage in actions that minimize bias. Or, if it's an individual, and that person isn't between you and your goal, move on.

Including Men Increases Women's Equality

In the warm, powerful American classic on racial inequality by Harper Lee, *To Kill a Mockingbird*, Atticus tells Scout:

"First of all," he said, "if you can learn a simple trick, Scout, you'll get along a lot better with all kinds of folks. You never really understand a person until you consider things from his point of view [...] until you climb into his skin and walk around in it.[27]*"*

There is such truth in what Atticus says that the first book in our leadership series, *Hidden in Plain Sight*[28], is devoted to how leaders can see the whole picture and from others' shoes. It is here that I believe women excel, looking beyond gender to see our shared interests and to help men see that horizon too.

The United Nations' UN Women launched the HeForShe.[29] campaign to engage men and boys as change agents for gender equality and women's rights. They need to be engaged, because men often control the resources—economic assets, political power, and the armed forces.[30] Equality impacts families and communities, the future of their daughters, and among the poor, survival. Equality can help them improve relationships with their spouses and their children, and in changing definitions of what constitutes masculinity, it can mean men will feel free to get the health care they need.[31]

International development organizations focused on gender engage prominent male leaders in communities to be change agents. They focus on helping educate young boys when their views about girls and women are forming. They work to relieve some of the economic and social pressures on men, so that men's behaviors, beliefs, and the cultural context influencing both can change too. There are no easy solutions, but there is progress that benefits us all.

I have listened to, read, and participated in policy and high-level discussions about reducing gender inequality. As an executive coach, I appreciate when high-level strategy is translated into how leaders think and interact on a day-to-day basis. That's why I found this tool from Catalyst immensely practical: *29 Actions Men Can Take to Create an Inclusive Workplace.*[32] It cites the pivotal role men can play with their behaviors and by being examples to other men. It suggests that doing ten actions from the list can really make a difference. They are **everyday actionable behaviors,** like listening to women, not telling or laughing at sexist jokes, or not humiliating other men who may behave in ways different from how you think a man should behave. The steps can't get much clearer than that, and they can be used to promote discussion among men.

Reflective Questions

Understanding the Larger Context: How Women Are Hidden Around the World

1. When you read about Malala Yousafzai and Microsoft's CEO, Satya Nadella, and what they are reflections of, what attributes do you think a woman needs to succeed in the corporate space and marketplace? For example, when I think about Malala, I think about courage. She was shot, received death threats and still continued to pursue her education and speak out about children's education. When I think about Satya Nadella's words, I think about how a woman needs to be aware that the playing field is uneven for women globally leading our businesses and our lives.

2. Where does your country rank in the World Economic Forum *Global Gender Gap Report?* If it's not in the top, how have you discovered ways to succeed in spite of, or perhaps because of factors that may not be favorable to women? Where do you have great hope for more equality, and how can you influence it as a leader?

3. Ask a woman who is a generation ahead of you about the changes she's experienced in women's rights. Ask someone who is two generations or even three ahead

of you about the changes she has noticed. Sometimes, we inherit rights that we take for granted, for example, the right to vote (if we have it) or the right to get credit (if we have it) in our own name. The right to vote in my country is only a few years older than my mother who is in her 90s. Have you seen things taking place now that mean more equality for girls and women?

4. Why is WEConnect International's work getting women businesses into global supply chains so important to women businesses, corporations, and the global economy? When you hear the phrase "Women as an emerging market" what do you think that means? Do you feel excited about this? Can you see how you are part of it and can help others emerge?

Blind Spots and Double Standards that Hide Women

5. People, whether male or female, and groups that have power can be blind to what it is like for those who don't. As you think about what you see around you, does this ring true? If you are in a position of power or influence, what are you doing, or can you do to include or advocate on behalf of those who aren't?

6. Sheryl Sandberg, Facebook's COO, said that "Women are perceived as too soft or too tough, but never just right, and as competent or likeable, but rarely both." If you've encountered this dilemma, how did you learn to navigate it successfully while being true to your own values and style? Who did you turn to—male or female—for guidance? What would you advise those you mentor or those new in the workforce to do?

7. In the corporate space, powerful women can have blind spots and behaviors that get in the way. If organizational gender bias is present, these behaviors can become career limiting. Do any of the four I mentioned sound like they may be true for you? For the first three, what trusted advisor or truth-teller can you have a candid, confidential conversation with and ask for his or her objective feedback? For the fourth, have you acknowledged how much stress you are under? Where can you get support? One thing I've seen in my clients and in my own life is that what happens outside work directly impacts work, and what happens at work directly impacts our lives outside it.

8. When I was a child, I got the message from my mother that my entrepreneurial venture selling flowers from my red Radio Flyer wagon wasn't ladylike. This message was underscored by the regional cultural norms at the time. Fast forward to starting my business. I had problems marketing and selling. When I could see my family's and my culture's influence, I could challenge the message I'd received. Marketing and selling became easier. What messages did you get in childhood and young adulthood about being a leader, promoting yourself, or selling?

When Men Are Hidden

9. Men have been called "the disposable sex" by Warren Farrell in the 1990s. They are the ones we send out to the field and to war. They frequently experience depression that they are acculturated not to talk about because it is perceived as a weakness. Gender can hide men too. How is gender hiding men in your organization or business?

Including Men Increases Women's Equality

10. There are men who don't recognize the inequalities between men and women, and others who want to preserve that inequality. Even when those mindsets directly impact you or others, how can you, male or female, be a gender diplomat—someone who educates and informs, someone who demonstrates respect for men by including them in the solution?

PART 2

When Gender is a Red Herring
that Hides Women

"You can't simply do a binary analysis (men versus women) when you want to look at the role of women on a complex issue…"

—Ed Carr
Associate Professor of Geography
University of South Carolina
Co-author of *Gender and Climate Change Adaptation in Agrarian Settings*[33]

When Ed Carr says you can't simply do a binary analysis, he is talking about how social markers like age, income, caste, and ethnicity come into play, as do country and regional differences. Likewise, we know we can't simply do a binary analysis when we are looking at women around the world. Let's take a look at how broad brush terms like "gender" and common beliefs can be red herrings that hide women.

Does a Masculine Society Hide Women?

If it truly is "a man's world," wouldn't it make sense that a masculine society (associated with men, of course!) is worse for women and a feminine one better? To test this, I chose Hofstede's cultural dimensions and did an analysis of the top and bottom 20 percent of countries from the *Global Gender Gap Report*.[34]

Geert Hofstede is a "Dutch social psychologist who did a pioneering study of cultures across modern nations.[35]" His cultural dimensions[36] are:

- Power Distance - a society's acceptance of inequalities in power.
- Individualism versus Collectivism - a society's preference for individuals to care for themselves or their families, or be cared for by others in exchange for blind loyalty.
- Masculinity versus Femininity and the *traits* associated with each. Masculine traits in a society represent a preference for achievement, heroism, assertiveness, and material reward for success. Feminine traits in a society represent a preference for cooperation, modesty, caring for the weak, and quality of life. A masculine society is more competitive, and a feminine one is more consensus-oriented.
- Uncertainty Avoidance - a society's comfort with uncertainty.
- Long-Term Orientation - a society's pragmatic future orientation versus a short-term conventional one.

Using Hofstede's Model, a "Masculine" or "Feminine" Society Makes Little Difference

Take a look at the **Masculinity** versus **Femininity** scores. There is very little difference for the top and bottom countries for women on the masculinity and femininity score. The top countries' score is 44.5 and the bottom countries' score is 47.1.

Hofstede's Masculinity/Femininity Dimension for Top & Bottom 20% of Countries for Women	
	Masculinity versus Femininity
Mean Top 20% Countries	44.5
Mean Bottom 20% Countries	47.1

Remember that a favorable environment for women in the *Global Gender Gap* Report is based on these key areas:

- Economic participation and opportunity
- Educational attainment
- Health and survival
- Political empowerment

So, just what does make a difference creating a favorable environment?

Where there is greater equality in power (where the **Power Distance** score is lower), and where individualism is emphasized (the **Individualism** score is higher), meaning the society prefers individuals to care for themselves or their families, the country is more favorable for women.

The **Power Distance** score for top countries is 44.8, meaning there is more equality in power. The score for the bottom countries is 71.9, meaning there is less equality in power. The **Individualism versus Collectivism** score for the top countries is 64.5, meaning individualism is emphasized, and the score for the bottom is 30.1, meaning collectivism is emphasized.

Hofstede's Cultural Dimensions for Top & Bottom 20% of Countries for Women		
	Power Distance	Individualism versus Collectivism
Mean Top 20% Countries	44.8	64.5
Mean Bottom 20% Countries	71.9	30.1

We Have Conflated
Male=Masculine and Female=Feminine

We have conflated the words male with masculine traits, and female with feminine traits. The pairings sound logical, don't they? In Hofstede's model, assertive is considered masculine and modest and caring, feminine. We all know men who are modest and caring and women who are assertive.

People recognized the terminology confusion. They renamed the masculine and feminine dimensions "Quantity of Life vs. Quality of Life."[37] These descriptors help avoid the mistake of conflating male/masculine and female/feminine.

We need to disconnect the behavioral attributes from the gender labels. The next exciting section reveals why.

An Alternate Universe Where Women Dominate and Men Don't Have Equal Rights

Let's take a look at a fascinating study[38] of the patriarchal Maasai society in Tanzania and the matrilineal Khasi in India, conducted by Uri Gneezy and John List. These two men are pioneers in conducting randomized field experiments out in the real world. You can read about their fascinating work in *The Why Axis: Hidden Motives and the Undiscovered Economies of Everyday Life*.

Gneezy and List describe walking into an alternate universe with the Khasi, where the power and control of resources are in women's hands, where men can't own property and there is even a men's movement for equal rights.

Are Women Innately Less Competitive?

Both Gneezy and List are parents of girls and consider their futures. They wanted to answer the question: "Do women make less money and occupy fewer management positions than their male counterparts because they are innately less competitive? Or do societal influences play a vital role in our competitive inclinations?"[39]

They carefully controlled variables during their field experiments to study competitiveness. Among the Maasai, the men competed more than the Maasai women. Among the Khasi, the women competed more than the Khasi men.

"Our study suggests that given the right culture, women are as competitively inclined as men, and even more so in many situations."

47

Further…

"The average woman will compete more than the average man if the right cultural incentives are in place."

It's not "a man's world." It's about the *social context* and *our acculturation*. More specifically, it's about which gender is the dominant competitor.

This is so exciting! It doesn't change the challenges women face in a "male as dominant competitor" society. **It gives women the chance to see the playing field.** In fact, Gneezy and List conducted another experiment that shows **when women know the rules of the game, for instance in a job announcement, they are more inclined to compete.** Consider these insights into the rules of the game.

The Origin of Deficit-Oriented Labels: The Confidence Debate

The debate about whether women aren't confident enough or are confident differently receives a lot of press—literally, in books, articles, and blogs. Several things are at play.

- **Women born into cultures where men are the dominant competitors often don't have as much practice at playing competitively.** Learning to compete, or as we'll see later, engaging in trade, builds trust and confidence.

- **When women's behavior differs from the cultural norm (for example, the dominant competitor behavior), they often get the message they have a deficit.** This is particularly prevalent in the corporate space. If a woman engages in the full range of behaviors that men do, she hits the double standard wall where men and women react negatively to her.

- **Women are confident differently.** It's a generalization, but women tend to see a bigger picture. Along with it comes an increased awareness of the impact on multiple stakeholders, power differentials, potential failures, and differences in skill levels.

What's a woman to do? Is there a way to succeed on this playing field in the corporate space or the marketplace? What will help her shine her brightest?

A Practical Mindset:
Engaging in the Trade Game

"DEFINITION of 'Trade:' A basic economic concept that involves multiple parties participating in the voluntary negotiation and then the exchange of one's goods and services for desired goods and services that someone else possesses." Source: www.investopedia.com

If you take on the **mindset of learning to play the trade game**, it becomes a series of transactions in the marketplace, and if you are internal to a company, in the corporate space. You no longer see yourself (or entertain anyone's assessment-direct or implied) as "not confident enough" or that you "don't take enough risks" or any other deficit-oriented label. It's a game to be entered into and where practice is important. You expect to lose some, win some, and learn. You understand there is a suite of skills to practice and to be cultivated. It's both competition and cooperation, and it's a way of engaging in continual learning and growth. It's where you are your boldest, most brilliant self, working with others to contribute to the world; however, *you* uniquely define contribution.

Anthropology Meets Adam Smith, Economist

A light bulb went off for me during a captivating conversation with Dr. Kevin McCabe. McCabe is the Founder and Co-Director of the Center for the Study of Neuroeconomics at George Mason University.[40] in Fairfax, Virginia, U.S.A. He is a neuroeconomist who studies the brain and how people make decisions in business contexts.

McCabe has conducted studies using functional magnetic resonance imaging (fMRI) to see what parts of the brain are involved in business decisions. He and his team run experiments like Trust Island and other games where the game objective is to earn money, to see how people play and respond when variables are controlled or changed.

We started talking about the role of trust in business.

The Impact of Trade on Trust and Practice

According to McCabe, **there is a growing proof that trading behavior increases trust**. "In other words," says McCabe, "I don't start trading because I trust you, but because it's necessary. Then later on, I become more trusting of people, because we succeeded in trading. As we become successful traders, we learn that people are not that bad, that basically they can be trusted more often than we thought."

Remember WEConnect International's CEO, Elizabeth Vazquez' comment? "...at the end of the day, trade is just people, that's all. People building relationships. Do I trust that you're going to give me what I ask for, and are you going to pay me what you say you're going to pay me?"

Moving beyond the gender trap means taking on the mindset of the "trade making game." It means going out into the marketplace (or corporate space) and engaging in transactions. The transactions may be highly complex[41] and nuanced depending on the corporate culture, politics, etc., or markets.

You move from the personal to the impersonal. It is no longer who you are or are not, as measured by a society where males are the dominant competitor. It is you engaging in the impersonal—the marketplace or corporate space.

You escape the trap of thinking challenges are directly tied to some deficit in you—real or imagined. You enter into the playing field ready to play. You are ready to practice, to learn, and to improve.

You engage in transactions and develop your trust in others. In turn, increasing trust through trading creates a virtuous cycle of trusting yourself more. You are cultivating your ability to learn and to lead.

Trading in the Corporate Space

Alex Cole was an executive at Cadbury.[42], a U.K. founded multinational and the second largest confectioner known for its chocolate, when she and a small group of people realized that the cocoa supply chain, with the aging cocoa trees and farmers, was not going to be able to supply the Cadbury of tomorrow. They were losing the product and the next generation of farmers.

Cole had to navigate a common, but complex leadership paradox in large companies: how to innovate while avoiding risk. She had three things in place that are crucial for navigating leadership paradox:

- A big, compelling vision that was worthy of her commitment.

- The authority and responsibility to address the challenges en route to her vision. She knew the company's bottom-line, and her own.

Cole and her team navigated this paradox creating a solution that supplied the Cadbury of the future and contributed to the sustainability of the cocoa growing communities. She had a masterful understanding of what her internal customer, the senior leadership, needed to make the best choice on behalf of the company and the farmers. She advises others to "seek forgiveness, not permission, but be within your rights." She thinks people second-guess themselves too often rather than just pushing as far as they can. If you get it wrong, then say, "I am sorry. I learned that lesson and it will not happen again."

She advises outlining the scenario, giving options that identify risks and upsides, and making recommendations along with the steps to take. You've got to assure them the company won't be going in blindly, but is going to have a better result by following your recommended path.

She offers two other tips for working with your internal customer:

- Have the informal conversations before the formal ones. Have conversations outside of the room informally, and know where the key players are going to come from when you have the formal ones.

• Don't be fixed on how you are going to get there, but have your point of conclusion. Socialize the idea; go to some random places as well as the obvious places to talk about it, but reach a point of conclusion where you can take action. Cole says you can get exactly what you want and probably do it faster and more effectively. She likens this strategy to, "float like a butterfly, sting like a bee."[43]

Reflective Questions

When Gender is a Red Herring That Hides Women

1. When I first began my research for this book, I wanted to discover where broad brush terms like "gender" and "gender equality" were red herrings (something that can be misleading) that prevent us from fully seeing women and men. For example, did you think that a masculine society would be less favorable to women? Were you surprised that the results from analyzing Hofstede's cultural model with the data from the World Economic Forum *Gender Global Gap Report* revealed that whether a society is "masculine" or "feminine" makes little difference?

2. Can you see where we've conflated "male=masculine" and "female=feminine?" Imagine how we can overlook men who are modest and caring—traits typically associated with female/feminine. There are

many. Or, how we can overlook women who are assertive—a trait typically associated with male/masculine. How would it change our societies' conversations if we stopped using the words "masculine" or "feminine" to describe character traits of men and of women?

An Alternate Universe Where Women Dominate and Men Don't Have Equal Rights

3. In the ground breaking research of Uri Gneezy and John List, we learn women are as competitive as men given the right culture. In most of the world, however, men are the dominant competitors. We also know from their research that once women know the rules of the game, they'll play. If it's a matter of learning to compete, what new ideas come to mind for leading in the marketplace or the corporate space?

4. Women often don't have as much practice competing as men. They get the message that they have a deficit when their behavior differs from cultural norms for men and women, and they are confident differently. If these ring true for you, what do you do that allows you to succeed? How would you advise those you mentor?

A Practical Mindset: Engaging in the Trade Game

5. If women can take on the practical mindset of the trade game—engaging in a series of transactions— whether they are in the corporate space or the marketplace, they will understand it is about practice and being in the game. The more you practice, the more you play, the more you trust others and yourself. If you take on the mindset of the trade game, where would business

get even easier for you? Where would you dare because it is a game (even when the stakes have an important social or business impact)? If you are already daring big, who can you share this mindset with to help them be at their leadership best?

PART 3

How to SHINE in the Corporate Space and in the Marketplace

In Part 1, we began with the big picture for women, the global context into which we are born, live, and lead. In Part 2, we learned how gender can be a red herring that hides both women and men. We illuminated the playing field with its implicit and explicit rules and discovered a practical, game-changing mindset.

In Part 3, we will translate these insights into high-level strategies and tools (action!) you can use to increase your impact. We'll begin with the differences between leading within a company—the corporate space—and leading a company in the marketplace. Then I'll share a Leadership Hand® model that gives you a systems view of your organization and that will help you make the most of the high level strategies to follow.

Differences in the Corporate Space and the Marketplace

Although there are overlaps, leading in the corporate space and leading your own business in the marketplace are different experiences. I've done both. Each has different strengths and challenges.

Globally, 90 percent of businesses[44] are small and medium-sized enterprises (SMEs). Most women-owned businesses are small, but that's changing even as I speak. Monica Smiley is the CEO and publisher of *Enterprising Women Magazine.*[45] The print and online magazine is devoted to helping women entrepreneurs grow their businesses, with a readership in 185 countries. Each year it holds an annual awards ceremony with a prestigious

Enterprising Women of the Year Award.[46] for different revenue categories. In 2015, Smiley said they had to create a new category: $100 million and above because there were so many women-owned businesses in that revenue category. This is exciting news.

Because so many women-owned businesses are SMEs, I am differentiating corporate space as mid-size to large corporations, and women-owned businesses as small to mid-size. No matter what size, you are likely to experience role pressure. By virtue of being in a leadership role, this is pressure you place on yourself (and others may too) to "know all the answers." Even if you intellectually understand that you can't, you can still fall prey to this.

The main differences in the corporate space where you are leading within or leading a mid-size to large one and owning your own business are:

- **Degree of autonomy and power.** When you join a mid-size to large company, it's like a marriage—you don't just marry a person (the position), you marry the person and his or her extended family system. Your power will be both direct and indirect. When you found your own business, you are creating your business family, and you will have more direct power within that particular context.

  How you experience the complexity differs as well. Within a mid-size to large company, you will have multiple internal and external stakeholders that create a complex set of influences. At the top of your own company, you deal with complexity, but it will more likely be external (the marketplace, your supply chain, governments, etc.).

- **Scope and scale of impact:** In a mid-size to large company, you can rise quickly through the corporate ranks or be hired into a position where your responsibility has a broad scope and scale of impact. It can take time to achieve these in your own business. But, when you do, it will be on your own terms.

- **How you define growth.** Growth in mid-size to large companies is often defined traditionally (e.g., market share, revenues, etc.). In small to mid-size companies, the definition of growth is unique to each business. It is usually a combination of a revenue goal with an equal or greater emphasis on a vibrant company culture and being an employer of choice—an employer that attracts and retains top talent.

Dev Technology Group, an award winning small technology business, is strikingly unique. It has repeatedly made a "Top Places to Work" list. It has an employee retention rate that exceeds the industry standard. Susie Sylvester, CEO and co-founder, places a premium on her organization's culture—a place where people enjoy who they work with, and do great work for their customers. She regularly invests in her leadership team's development. This has the direct benefit of strengthening the culture. In turn, it lays a healthy foundation as the company enters into a period of rapid, dramatic growth.

The Big Picture: A Leadership Hand®
Development Model

I've found the following model helpful when working with clients on their individual, their leadership team's, and employees' development because it takes a **systems view.** That, and the fact that humans do beautifully when they go from an abstract concept like leadership development and turn it into a simple visual model. We see how the parts interrelate, and we can focus on specific components.

At the top of the triangle is the Vision, "You" is in one corner and "Team" in another. In the center is an inverted triangle with the words "Learning While Doing." It would be easy to add to this by drawing concentric circles around it: an inner circle for customers and clients, a larger circle for the industry—competitors, supply chains, etc.—and the largest circle for the global economy.

We're going to focus on the most powerful leverage point: you. That's the "You" in model.

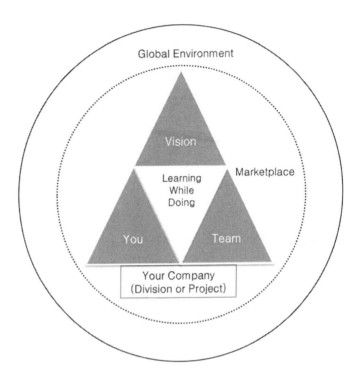

Leadership Hand® Development Model

High Level Strategies to SHINE
in the Corporate Space and in the Marketplace

Remember the mindset of engaging in trade as a game? That's where you move beyond the gender trap or any other trap by engaging in a series of transactions, whether trading in the actual marketplace or "trading" within the corporate space. The very act of engaging in trading increases trust in yourself and in the marketplace—those with whom you engage.

Because it's the **game** of trade, you expect to lose some, win some, and learn. Unless we had a lot of brothers or played competitive sports, most of us didn't learn to engage in business or leadership this way. We didn't learn to compete or to embrace failure and feedback. If we did, we still had to find our own unique way of doing so, and we were likely still influenced by our gender.

Once you embrace this mindset, you need high level strategies to help you shine even brighter. These strategies will amplify your abilities and your impact. Are they set in stone? No. Put them into practice, tweak them as you go, and make them your own.

Each has sound roots in my work with men and women leaders from Fortune 500 companies to small and mid-size companies, helping them develop their leadership skills to achieve business results. While men benefit powerfully from them too, they work with and leverage traits I've observed in women.

See your big, compelling vision on the horizon.

Have a strategic framework to help you stay mentally focused and minimize distractions.

Investigate, Explore, Innovate—learn how to learn.

Notice your bold brilliance, and help others notice theirs.

Embrace failure and feedback. These mean you are in the game, not on the sideline.

S: See Your Big, Compelling Vision (BCV) on the Horizon

What is it you want to accomplish in your lifetime in the best of all worlds? What difference are you making for your family, for your employees, for your customers, for an underserved population or the world? From this, describe the big, compelling vision (BCV) you see on the horizon in **three to five years**. Why only three to five years when it can take ten, twenty, or more? Three to five years makes it more concrete and within reach. The vision and seeing the big picture is so important that I devoted the first book in the *Hidden Stakeholders, Hidden Solutions* series to this Leadership Hand® approach.[47].

Women seem most inspired, resilient, and determined when their vision serves others. If you want the most enlivened vision for your business and those you lead, make sure you state who is being served.

Because women generally place more emphasis on a healthy corporate culture, and because a big, compelling vision is infused with your deeply held values, it will:

- Help align your employees.
- Attract the right talent.
- Contribute to brand strength as your company, division, or directorate evolves.

The vision Charito Kruvant, CEO and co-founder of Creative Associates International[48] had was "to support people around the world to realize the positive change they seek." When she went to the bank for a loan, she was turned down because she was a woman. Kruvant immediately got a man to go with her. The bank's treatment of her was a mere detail: she had her eye on something far more important—her big, compelling vision.

Kruvant and her company have faced many challenges that are part and parcel of being in business, along with the challenges of breaking new ground in the development industry as a woman-owned, women-led business. Today her company has helped communities and people in 85 developing countries "improve education, stabilize neighborhoods, and enhance community resiliency." It is a leader in the international development arena, and has grown in size to $100m USD. This is the power of a big, compelling vision that serves others.

Remember the big, compelling vision Alex Cole had as an executive at Cadbury? It was to supply the Cadbury of the future, and contribute to the sustainability of the cocoa growing communities. That vision supported Cole in navigating the complexity of working with internal stakeholders and within the context of what is typical for large, mature companies—an aversion to risk. She led from within and did so successfully.

Ensuring Your Business Model Serves the Vision: What You Can Learn from Elizabeth Vazquez

Organizations can lose sight of those they are trying to serve and how to serve them best. Vazquez was able to step back and recognize WEConnect's business model wasn't serving the vision. It created barriers for the very women business owners they wanted to reach. She made the bold, necessary move of changing the model her organization was founded on—the very one she'd argued for with powerful stakeholders.

Make sure your business hasn't lost sight of whom you are serving.

• Ask yourself, what is our big, compelling vision today? Is it current? Currency means looking at how you, your team, and organization have grown. It means looking at how the marketplace, your customers, and clients have evolved.

• You must get feedback from your customers (internal or external). Better yet, incorporate the customer development approach of lean start-ups where ongoing customer input directly shapes the creation and evolution of products and services. For another extraordinary example of working with customers and stakeholders, read Paul Polak's story in *Hidden by Your Customer: How to See People, Profits and Solutions*. Polak is on a mission for business as a solution to poverty for those living on $2 a day.

H: Have a Strategic Framework to Help You Focus

One of the biggest challenges of leading within an organization or leading your business is distraction. You can fell prey **to environmental distractions**, for example, people knocking on your door, emails, phone calls, or anything that causes you to change mental gears to address it. There are **behavioral distractions** where your time management, prioritizing, or strategic thinking skills may need to improve.

There are **strategic distractions** that take you off-course, or spread you too thin, diluting your resources and impact. Entrepreneurs (male and female) in small, growing businesses can fail to monetize existing services and products by making fundamental course changes (a pivot) too often.

Women excel at managing multiple initiatives and can take on too much. A one-page **strategic framework** can help you:

- Stay focused on what's important.
- Leverage your resources wisely.
- Delegate better.

- Make sound strategic decisions about new opportunities, staying the course or changing direction.

It can assist with, but won't take the place of, time management skills if you need those. When you look at your strategic framework, you are automatically working "on your business and not in it."[49]

I refer to mine regularly. Every time a shiny, new idea comes along (which is frequent!), I remind myself to stick with what I've picked. I call it my **"pick and stick strategy."** Is the shiny, new idea consistent with our annual strategic framework and what we determined was a priority at the inception of the new year? **Most of the time, even though it's a really great idea, I need to stay the strategic course to maximize my business's impact and return.**

If I'm really considering investing in the new idea, I revisit the assumptions made when we completed the framework. Are they still valid or is there new evidence that means they need to be revised? An important guide on how to identify and work with assumptions can be found in *Hidden by Assumptions: Seeing People & Solutions for Your Important Business Issues.*

Your framework should fit on **one page**. An advisory board, board of directors, or a mentor can help you think this through. Here are the elements to include:

- **Vision (3 to 5 years)** – Describe in a couple of sentences.
- **Annual Focus** – What's the most important focus for the year to bring that vision to life? Is it

increased sales, growing your leadership team, diversification, or building your brand?

- **Strategic Mindset** – What's the single-most important mindset **you** need to bring your vision to life? Is it a mindset of positive expectancy? Is it calm resolve that every setback is a springboard to success?

- **Behavior/s** – What one or two behaviors do **you** personally need to engage in daily to bring your vision to life? Is it setting aside time at the beginning and end of each week to reflect? Is it growing your leadership team so you can focus on the strategic?

- **Top Three Objectives** - What are the top 3 objectives that if you achieved them this year would bring this vision to life or powerfully accelerate your progress? Yes, I mean it—only three. In *The Four Disciplines of Execution: Achieving Your Wildly Important Goals*, authors Chris McChesney and Sean Covey advocate for only one. It can be painful to prune the list, but the thinking that has to go into it and the prioritizing will be invaluable. When you go beyond three, I have bad news: the less likelihood any will be achieved.

- **Quarterly Projects** – Drawing from the 3 annual objectives, what projects need to take place to reach the objectives? A project can be carried over into subsequent quarters.

- **Month-To-Month Project or Components** – Drawing on the quarterly projects, what are the month-to-month projects or project components?

Use this high-level guide to evaluate your progress periodically. That can be quarterly or every six months. As you look back at the beginning of the year, do the objectives make sense or does something need to change? What assumptions did you make then? Do they still hold true, or do you have new information? Most likely, your strategy for accomplishing the objectives is what needs to be adjusted. Do it. Just be thoughtful and reasoned about it. **Being too agile can make your company fragile.**

I: Investigate, Experiment, Innovate
Learn How to Learn

"Life is the great experiment. Each of us is an experiment of one - observer and subject - making choices, living with them, recording the effects."

—George Sheehan, M.D.
Returned to running at age 45

Learn how to learn. Athletes are in a continual process of experimenting, noticing what works, and tweaking it. As a leader, you need to know how to investigate, experiment, and innovate to be at your best. It is *learning how to learn.*

Have you ever heard the phrase, "How we do one thing is how we do everything?" Put yourself in different contexts to observe your patterns. Traveling in different countries and cultures is a great way to experiment and observe. For example, what did you do when you were lost or things broke down? Where did you make limiting assumptions or ones that allowed you to stay open and receptive? Can you see how these same patterns are showing up in your leadership style?

One of my most powerful business strategies came from when I had a broken ankle and could not run. Running was my major physical, mental, emotional, and social outlet. A lot got disrupted. I would lament to one of my mentors, Suzi Tucker.[50]. She kept saying, "find another way." That made no sense. How do you find another way to run when you can't?

One day, I had a "tiny aha!" I realized moving was what was most important, not just how I moved. In pretty short order (ankle-healing time) it led to me training in multi-sport where you swim, bike, and run. That led to me completing my first international distance triathlon, followed by a Half Ironman—a 1.2 mile (1.9 km) swim, a 56 mile (90 km) bike ride, and a 13.1 mile (21.1 km) run completed back to back. It was glorious weather and one of the most fun days I've had in my life.

I, with help from Tucker, learned how to learn. Now, when there are business setbacks, I step back to ask "what's most important?" Am I fixated on the means (running) versus the outcome that's even more important, like being in joyful motion?

Learn in Community. For many of us, me included, our roles can be solitary ones. It's not because we don't have others around us. It's where we stand as leaders. We are at the helm looking out on the horizon. We are responsible for the whole—our own business, a company, a division, or directorate. That position and all the work we know there is to do can mean we overlook a basic human and essential business need: our social and community needs.

At a celebration of International Women's Day, Gina Reiss-Wilchins, then-Director, Girl Up, United Nations

Foundation[51], said that one in ten girls in Ethiopia does not have a friend. It made my heart break. For the young girl, it is literally about surviving. If she is among the hardest-to-reach girls in the world and has a friend, it increases the likelihood she stays in school, finds work, learns life skills, and participates in community and civic life.

For women in business, being connected is a qualitatively different experience but it, too, is about surviving and thriving. In a business community, whether it's a women's association, an annual event like the Enterprising Women Awards Celebration where women entrepreneurs around the globe come together, or a private women's business group, you will learn from others and feel relief to hear that your challenges are common—that it's not just you or your organization.

You will receive support that helps you and your organization thrive. You will get to give support to others and experience the fulfillment that comes with it. These are opportunities for what Susan RoAne[52], speaker and coach, whose book *How to Work a Room* has sold over one million copies, calls **Mentors of the Moment (M.O.M.s)**—informal mentoring moments that can occur at any time and from anyone.

I am an advocate for learning communities that are in-person events. Nothing can take their place. However, there are resources that can complement in-person meetings, or be an uplifting alternative. Here are two resources created by women's advocates that shine a light on other women, their courage, and wisdom.

- The book *Vital Voices: The Power of Women Leading Change Around the World* written by Alyse Nelson, the CEO of Vital Voices Global Partnership is one. She shares story after story of remarkable, world-changing women. For many, in the most difficult circumstances, the light she shines keeps them alive. Their detractors know these women are being seen, and they have the support of the international community. As you read each story, connect with your own courage and conviction. You are not alone, and you are making a difference.

- The j. jane Project[53], founded by Jessica Jane Stepleton Stern, is one that you can access online. The j. jane Project was created to inspire mentorship between women. It is a collection of interviews from women around the world that reflects their personal and professional experience, different socioeconomic backgrounds, and various paths taken, "all exposing a common thread: a thread of grace." The interviews are like having an intimate, in-person conversation with someone sharing her unvarnished, wise worldview.

N: Notice Your Own Bold Brilliance - A Glorious Practice

Smart, competent women regularly overlook their unique, bold brilliance. Sometimes we have an inkling, but we really just can't see ourselves in all our glory. Our acculturation as females and our ability to see the big picture, where we excel at discerning others strengths, all play a part. We can be hidden from ourselves. This is true for even the most accomplished leaders. Here are the patterns I see most frequently:

- You're so good at what you do, you don't think twice about it much less notice it.
- You're focused on where you are going. There's so much more to be accomplished, you haven't even paused to see what you just navigated brilliantly.
- You're in the habit of giving credit to others.
- You haven't had a simple practice that lets you see, feel and hear your unique, bold brilliance.

At a women's leadership group in a Fortune 500 company, I led a Bold & Brilliant session. I asked participants to find a time big or small when they were bold and brilliant and share their story with another person. The energy in the room soared.

One woman had helped a client during the sale of his business, which was very personal to him. She shared the story with the group, from the challenges she helped him address to the happy results. Everyone broke out in applause. She never fully realized just how amazing what she'd done was until others listened. She could see her brilliance reflected in our appreciative listening.

Bold & Brilliant Exercise. Please give yourself the gift of ten to twenty minutes to do this exercise. You can do it solo, but I recommend you do it with someone else. Consider it a gift exchange—and it really is.

1. Think of at least three times when you were at your most bold and brilliant. This can be at work, at play, with friends or family. It can be large with a big impact or a small, private triumph that took place in a single conversation. Scan last week or the past quarter.

You get to decide what constitutes bold and brilliant. It has a wide, wide range. Jot down a few key words to describe each example.

2. Choose one and write a short paragraph describing it. It doesn't matter which. Don't overthink it. If you really like one, choose that one. What were you doing and with whom? What was the challenge, and what was the result? Describe how you it made you feel.

3. Share it with someone else. Ask the person to listen appreciatively but not to evaluate or give advice. You are offering the person a gift by sharing it, and you are receiving one—you're really being listened to.

4. Notice what it feels like in your body. You should be feeling increased energy and confidence. Really notice—your backbone, breathing, posture, and face. When you think, write, and talk about and embody your bold and brilliant experience, you are helping wire neurons together. The more you notice and practice, the quicker you'll have access to thoughts, feelings, and emotions of you at your best.

5. If there was a "tiny aha" of insight from what you noticed in your story, what was it? Was it that you dared even when you were afraid? Was it that you helped improve people's lives? Was it that you trusted your gut when the "facts" said no, and your gut was right?

6. Take turns with your partner. If you are doing this with someone else, you can each do steps 1 and 2. After you've done those, each person takes a turn sharing his or her story. Again, the listener's job is to listen deeply and appreciatively. No advice.

If you want to turn this into a practice, find someone willing to engage in it say once a week for a month. You could also put a reminder on your calendar to reflect at the end of week, month, or quarter.

Gather up your bold brilliances. Bring them with you as you move forward.

> ### Your Personal Brand: Standing Out Is Essential
>
> There's a wonderful phrase I learned from Alan Weiss when I attended his Million Dollar Consulting College®: "You must make the first sale to yourself." He meant that you must first believe in your own value before you can expect to sell to clients or customers. Noticing your own bold brilliance lays a solid foundation to make that first sale (and even bigger sales!) to yourself. Once you've done that, how do you then let your bold, brilliance, and belief in yourself inform your personal brand?
>
> That's where Dorie Clark, an expert on marketing and branding, comes in. In her wildly popular book *Stand Out: How to Find Your Breakthrough Idea and Build a Following Around It*[54], she states that standing out is no longer an option; it's essential. Clark says you must find the breakthrough idea that sets you apart, build a following around it, choose strategies to create thought leadership, and then be intentional about making a living at it. She isn't merely advocating self-

promotion. It's about making your contribution to the world, and vitalizing your business or career. Sound familiar? Yes, these are the same drivers for this book.

E: Embrace Failure and Feedback

Failing = learning. Failing means being in the game. Failure, the kind that says you haven't hit the mark, is just feedback.

Sara Blakely, Founder of Spanx, is the youngest self-made billionaire and the first female billionaire to sign Bill Gates' and Warren Buffett's Giving Pledge[55]. Of the world's richest people, those who sign it pledge to donate at least half of their wealth to charities. (Go read Blakely's letter.) Blakely said:

"My dad encouraged us to fail. Growing up, he would ask us what we failed at that week. If we didn't have something, he would be disappointed. It changed my mindset at an early age, that failure is not the outcome, failure is not trying. Don't be afraid to fail."

If you didn't grow up competing, you may not know how to fail fast, and embrace failing as part of learning. Most societies (our institutions and families) focus on success as an outcome rather than success as the satisfaction in the effort. Carol Dweck wrote a standout book on this called *Mindset: The New Psychology of Success*. If you are focused only on the outcome, fear of failing can keep you from trying. Failure doesn't need to be heavy and destabilizing. In fact, the more you practice competing, daring, and taking risks, the more you will find yourself embracing it for the increased resolve and surge of energy it brings.

Helping Your Team and Employees SHINE

I conducted interviews with a dozen women CEOs who own technology businesses. The companies ranged in size from under $1m USD to $100m USD operating in national and international markets. The conversations illuminated what I'd already observed in women leaders: **it's not just where their company is going, it's how they get there.** For women leaders, the two are tightly integrated.

The "how" rests on a foundation of:

- Cultivating a healthy organizational culture.
- Being a great place to work.
- Becoming a brand known and trusted by customers, clients, and strategic partners.

To accomplish these and other important objectives, you can bring SHINE to your leadership team and employees. Here are guidelines for applying them in a team setting.

See *your big, compelling vision on the horizon.*

Engage them in your big, compelling vision. Create a draft and ask for their input. It will bring new energy to your team. A skilled facilitator, whether in-house or external, can be an excellent investment for creating a truly shared vision. He or she can help facilitate discussions so that everyone comes to a shared understanding, and help you craft a meaningful, clear vision statement.

Remember that the vision is where deeply held values reside, which is so important to women leaders, particularly those who founded their own businesses. A big, compelling vision energizes and unifies everyone. It pulls everyone forward when setbacks occur. It's the first place I start with clients.

Share the vision with everyone—when all employees come together, at awards events, when hiring employees, when you are on a panel or the keynote speaker at a conference. Tell the story of how it came to be. Your story will help increase the sense of community with internal and external stakeholders. It will uplift and engage others.

*H*ave a strategic framework to help you stay mentally focused and minimize distractions.

You and your team can complete a one-page strategic framework together focused on your company, your directorate, or division. Allow employees to discuss it and ask questions. They will see where their and others' functions fit in the big picture. Discussing fit, priorities, etc. will result in sharing information, knowledge, and unleashing energy that might otherwise go untapped. A skilled facilitator is useful here. If you don't have access to a facilitator and have a group where everyone will speak up, the one-page format and its structure does a good job helping your group self-facilitate.

Make sure you identify and capture your assumptions.[56] Doing so will assist you in assessing when or if to adjust your priorities as the year progresses. When you do this and revisit them, it will enhance your leadership team's ability to learn how to learn.

*I*nvestigate, Explore, Innovate—learn how to learn.

While your individual development is the strongest leverage point for having a bigger impact and making a contribution, the second strongest is your team's development. You can be a strong leader and still have a team that needs strengthening, and vice versa. That has huge implications for what you can accomplish for your team members' and your organization's future.

When you have articulated the big, compelling vision, what are the day-to-day behaviors each of you need to engage in as a team to bring it to life? Can you describe those in a way someone could actually tell whether you are engaging in them or not? That's important. Otherwise, a concept or idea stays abstract. For example, "we respect each other's time" is a great guideline but can have different meanings for different people. Translating it into a specific behavior, like "we are on time for meetings" is crystal clear.

How will you know you're doing a good job with the behaviors? What positive feedback mechanism can you regularly engage in that affirms where you are doing right and well, and what needs to change? **Your team must integrate insight and action with the vision and objectives in sight.** That's the "Learning While Doing" piece of the Leadership Hand® Development Model.

Annual retreats to explore what you learned the year past and how you want to apply it to the year ahead are invaluable opportunities. Done right, they go from knowledge sharing to what I call "wisdom sharing." Talk about a power tool for building culture and a brand that shines. This is it.

Expensive in the Short Run, High Returns in the Long Run: What You Can Learn from Harriet Lamb, CEO, Fairtrade International

Fairtrade International[57] helps farmers who grow coffee, tea, and cotton, and gold miners achieve fairer trading conditions, gain more influence over their futures, and promotes sustainability. Its work involves a diverse set of stakeholders with varied interests—from small producers to major multinational brands, and everyone up and down that supply chain. Adding further complexity are the distinctions in regional views—one view in Africa, another in Latin America, and the interdependencies in the trade ecosystem.

A conversation with farmers that starts with chocolates quickly means having to talk to the sugar farmers and then the cocoa farmers, the companies, and then the traders. The individual conversations are important but to bring all those conversations together means bringing people together. CEO, Harriet Lamb, says this is crucial. She is convinced that when crossing cultures and languages meeting in person is the only way. I agree. I find this true whether crossing cultures, crossing functions or addressing any complex, important challenge. If you're going to fully engage people and unleash their talent, it's going to cost money in the short run. (As one African farmer said

> to Lamb "Democracy is expensive.") The cost of not doing so is even higher in the long run.

Notice your bold brilliance, and help others notice theirs.

The Bold & Brilliant exercise works beautifully with groups and teams. You can also ask your leadership team to do this with their direct reports.

A word of caution: if there's been a breakdown in trust or respect at any level in the organization, an exercise alone isn't going to rebuild it. It may just make people angry.

If you have access to an organizational development specialist, conduct a Bold & Brilliant survey with all employees. You could adapt this using a process called Appreciative Inquiry. Be sure to respect confidentiality, share high-level themes with everyone, determine next steps, and of course, follow-through on them.

Embrace failure and feedback. Failure=learning.

Remember Sara Blakely? Her father asked her each week what she'd failed at with the expectation that she do so and embrace it. It paid off with an extraordinarily successful product and brand.

What incentives have you set up that reward experimentation and thus, failure for your team and employees? One organization celebrates the most outrageous failure each year. A well-known tech firm allows employees a percentage of time each week to pursue any interest they have. How are you encouraging your shining stars to embrace failure as part of learning?

Two Special Situations:
Taking a Stand, or Wanting to Give Up

These next two sections address special situations: when to take a stand on an important issue, and what to do when we are ready to give up.

When to Take a Stand Whether Against Gender Bias or Something Else...

I was speaking to a group of leaders in a multinational company. Someone asked, "what if taking a stand causes issues?" Taking a stand always causes issues. Whether it's against double standards or something else, what's the cost to you if you don't?

I fervently believe some part of us is always on the lookout for when we will take a stand on our own behalf or on behalf of our deeply held values. Usually, your gut intuition has the best understanding of the cost if you don't. Cost can be hard to quantify, but that gut intuition knows even when you don't have words to explain its logic.

- In Mexico, women who stand up against the drug cartels using social media may lose their lives if their identities are discovered. They are taking a stand for their children, their communities, and their future.

- In 1965, Annie Lee Cooper, an African American civil rights activist, wanted to register to vote in Texas. The sheriff prodded her in the neck with a billy club, and she punched him in the jaw. She was thrown to the ground while the sheriff beat her. She took a stand for her civil rights and more.

- In a Costa Rican village, men were leaving the community to find work. The women wondered what to do to maintain their community and to earn a living. Without any experience, they founded La Asociación de Mujeres Organizadas de Biolley (ASOMOBI) and began the first woman-owned coffee micro mill in Costa Rica. In A Small Section of the World.[58], a film featuring these entrepreneurs, Ana Laura Quirós Montoya, a founding partner, said men told them "you should be cooking, not growing coffee." Without engaging in an argument that would distract from the bigger business goal, her response was simple: "We do both."

In her book *Bossypants*, comedian Tina Fey, a Saturday Night Live television writer and actor who produced and starred in *30 Rock*, tells a story about her colleague Amy Poehler. Poehler told a vulgar "unladylike" joke. Jimmy Fallon, another popular comedian, told her in a mock-voice to 'Stop that. It's not cute. I don't like it."

I was listening to the audio edition (a must if you are a Tina Fey fan). The world seemed to stand still as I heard Fey say Poehler "went black in the eyes for a second, and wheeled around on him." "I don't [expletive] care if you like it."[59] Now, that is taking a stand, and one that rises up from the core. Poehler meant business and didn't give a damn what others thought.

Fey offers this:

"When faced with sexism, ageism or lookism or even really aggressive Buddhism, ask yourself the following question: Is this person between me and what I want to do?"

If the answer is no, ignore it and move on. If the answer is yes and it's your boss, she advocates trying to find someone above your boss, who isn't a jerk, or find a neutral proving ground to focus on.

If you are working within a large company or want to shift an industry culture, I think it's wise to pick your battles. *Be strategic.* Don't win the battle to lose the war. Babcock and Laschever's advice in their book, *Ask For It: How Women Can Use the Power of Negotiation to Get What They Really Want,* is to be "relentlessly pleasant" to avoid triggering a like bias from both men and women. There are cultural norms, and they are powerful. My point here isn't that you subjugate yourself or be inauthentically compliant, it is that you should know what is most important to you and choose wisely.

If You Are Ready to Give Up…
What I Learned from a Vision Quest

I didn't know what was next in my life or where or how to make my greatest contribution. For all intents and purposes, I had a great job: autonomy, influence, scope and scale of responsibility, job security, and a career path. But, something was missing…

I decided to go on a vision quest, a Native American spiritual ritual for discerning one's life purpose. I traveled to Nevada and set out with a small group for ten days in Death Valley. We came together for meals, but I spent most of the day alone in quiet reflection. On day six, I set out on a three-day fasting solo. The final night of the solo, I was to create a medicine wheel, a stone circle, and to stay up all night within it. It signified staying with my life.

It was so beautiful standing on the desert floor with the mountains in the distance. There were only rocks, a rattlesnake or two, and gently creaking creosote bushes—no other person in sight. I made my medicine wheel using large stones to mark the major compass points. Almost an afterthought, I sprinkled small white stones along the periphery.

I remember asking for guidance that night: "What's next? How do I make my greatest contribution?"

Two things helped me stay in my wheel and awake—helped me stay with my life. In the dim light, I couldn't see the big stones, even looking directly at them.

- The small white stones, visible only in my peripheral vision, reflected the tiniest bit of moonlight, helping me stay in my wheel.
- When I reached the point of greatest fatigue, I said, "I get it. I must stay with my life. But now, I can't stay up anymore. I'm lying down to sleep." It was bitterly cold—too cold to sleep.

When the light dawned, I felt a sense of triumph. I'd stayed awake and in my wheel. That vision quest taught me a lot about what was to come in life and business. Your big, compelling vision is your North Star, but sometimes **it's the little things in the periphery that guide you**. Sometimes **what presented itself as your**

biggest problem becomes the resource that helps you achieve an important objective.

Oh yes... In less than a year's time, I discovered a new path, which led to founding my business, Leadership Hand, providing leadership development to leaders and their teams. It's in the role of CEO of my company that I speak to you today.

Executive Summary

My work in the leadership development field, and my resounding belief in women and business as a force for global good, compelled me to write this book, *Hidden by Gender*.

It is intended for women in countries with sufficient political stability and economic infrastructure to allow them to focus on leading within a company or in their own business, whether a Fortune 500 company, a small and medium enterprise (SME), or a small and growing business (SGB).

If we were talking in person, I would tell you with depth and feeling just how important it is for you to be your boldest, most brilliant self—for you, for those you lead—for women and men, girls and boys around the world.

I had a personal need, too, in writing this. It was the need to understand how being female has influenced me as a leader. There were times when I couldn't see the playing field, didn't know what the game was, or how to play it. Today, I have solid answers that I didn't have early in my career or when I founded my business fifteen years ago. I'm still clearly on the journey with you.

Hidden by Gender starts with the big picture, **the global context into which women are born, live, and lead. It's an unequal world.** Most women have no choice but to focus on surviving. Even when her survival isn't at stake, a woman's rights aren't guaranteed. When they are, and she is leading her own business, she will still have challenges getting access to credit, training, business networks, and opportunities. When she is leading within a company, she'll likely be held to double standards and have to figure out the hidden playing field with its implicit and explicit rules.

But gender can be a red herring that hides both men and women. We've conflated the words "masculine," associated with assertive = male, and "feminine," associated with modest and caring = female. Surprisingly, whether a society is "masculine" or "feminine" makes little difference to how favorable a country is for women. Fascinating research by Uri Gneezy and John List reveals that women with the right cultural incentives in place are just as competitive as men. What determines competiveness (and success) is who the society's dominant competitor is, whether male or female.

Two other conversations led to major insights. The first was with Dr. Kevin McCabe, a neuroeconomist, who talked about how trading behavior increased trust. The second was my conversation with WEConnect International CEO Elizabeth Vazquez who said:

"…at the end of the day, trade is just people, that's all; people building relationships. Do I trust that you're going to give me what I ask for, and are you going to pay me what you say you're going to pay me?"

These conversations led to two fundamental insights:

1. The playing field is not about male/female; it's about who is the dominant competitor. "Competitor" is the key word. For most of the world, males are the dominant competitors.

2. If women adopt the mindset of playing the trade game, whether from a leadership position within a company or leading their own enterprise, they understand the need to compete and the role of

practice. They expect to win some and to lose some. Further, as they engage in the trade game, their trust in others and in themselves increases.

The last part of *Hidden by Gender* notes the differences between the corporate space and the marketplace. It presents a Leadership Hand® development model to help see you, your team, and organization more clearly. It offers five high level strategies and tools to help you leverage women's unique leadership traits. The first guideline is to have a big, compelling vision. The second is to use a strategic framework to help you stay focused throughout the year. The third is the most important life and leadership skill you can have: learning how to learn. The fourth is a practice that reveals your brilliance. The fifth is the perfect capstone: embracing failure and feedback. There is a section on how to apply each with your leadership team so that you and your team shine.

Take what you read and make it your own. Discover and reveal your boldest, most brilliant self. As a woman, as a leader, you're a beautiful work of art. Go forth and shine!

Beth Hand, CEO
Leadership Hand LLC

And Finally,
What's One Tiny Aha You Can Act on Right Now?

What's one "tiny aha" you got from this book that you can take action on *right* now? The quicker you can get that action on your calendar—what I call a "calendar moment" to make a phone call, schedule a meeting, or send an email, **the quicker you can accelerate the benefits of your thinking and learning here.**

Free Guide

As a special thank you for your interest in *Hidden by Gender*, the sixth book in our series, we've created a free downloadable guide to accompany it. You can find it here:

www.leadershiphand.com/freegenderguide

Thank You

Thank you for reading and exploring this Leadership Hand® book. It, like each book in the *Hidden Stakeholders, Hidden Solutions*, has a core premise: when we fully see all stakeholders, we discover powerful solutions to our business and leadership challenges.

If you enjoyed this book, please write a review on Amazon. These are vital to a book's success. They help others decide whether to buy it, and they offer your unique thoughts about the book, ideas, or strategies you found particularly helpful.

You can also visit Amazon for other books in the series. They are short, focused on a powerful leadership competency, and enlivened by wonderful real-life examples of leaders whose work contributes to global good. I've deconstructed their brilliance so that you can use it to enhance your own brilliance or draw from it outright. You'll get simple models to illustrate points and to guide you as you put the principles into practice.

Hidden in Plain Sight! Rapidly Discovering Solutions for Your Business & Leadership Issues

Hidden by Assumptions: Seeing People & Solutions for Your Important Business Issues

Hidden by the C-Suite: How to Find Solutions for Your Business Challenges by Including People

Hidden by Leadership Paradox: How to Navigate to Solutions in Between

Hidden by Your Customer: How to See People, Profits and Solutions

Acknowledgements

The journey that inspired this book began before I was born.

I am grateful to my father. He instilled in me a passion for learning and a love of the outdoors. As a child, I remember fishing with Dad for jumping mullet with handlines that trailed off the stern of the old Crosby, an outboard engine boat.

As a young adult, I spent long, exquisite days with him fishing for marlin in the deep blue of the Atlantic Ocean Gulf Stream, the Bahamas, and Costa Rica, on Bertram sportfishing boats, and on the smooth riding Buddy Davis. In an instant, I can imagine sitting on the cottage porch, salt breeze blowing, waves breaking on the shore, with Dad beside me, both of us in rocking chairs watching Bogue Sound, replete with the sense that life is good. I miss you, Dad.

It was his passion for learning in small ways and large that inspired my path today: he was part of a study group devoted to his profession, an avid reader, and invested in business consultants to work with him and his staff.

I am grateful to my mother. At 92 years of age, she continues to navigate the paradox of breaking gender rules while following them. Because of her, we grew up with all kinds of creatures. My brother's two favorite Bantam chickens named Chicken Salad and Drumstick… Ernest, the tiny caiman and crocodile look-alike that my sister brought home… Cats, dogs, baby quail, ducks, parakeets, a cockatiel, a rabbit, a horse… Life is whole with animals in it. She's taught me the importance of the right tools and how to use them to maintain a yard. (Who knew it would influence me getting certified to use a chain saw so I could help clear forest trails!)

She and my father sparked my interest in a bigger world through travel, study, and work in different countries.

Anne Aden, thank you for gracing my life with who you are as a person and as a friend. Saint Dave, you are a treasured part of my life. Friends and guides, Suzi Tucker and Pat Collins, you are for me and for so many others, what Miracle Gro® is for flowers.

Laurel Bartlett[60], you have provided clarity to this series and the publishing process. You've been a place of calm amidst my many commitments. Joanne Lozar Glenn[61], what you taught me over many years as I wrote the *Written by Hand©* newsletter laid the foundation for this work. Thank you to Sara Martinez[62] for bringing both heart and mind to the Spanish translation. Thank you Kholoud H.[63] for your work translating the Arabic version, and Alia El Mohandes for your support and counsel.

And finally, to affectionate, exuberant Sam: you aren't always a good dog, but you are a great one.

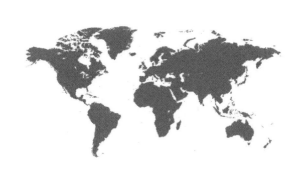

WE HELP MISSION DRIVEN LEADERS
ACHIEVE STRATEGIC RESULTS

Leadership Hand LLC serves mission-driven leaders and teams in small, mid-size to Fortune 500 companies, and international development enterprises. We offer organizational and leadership development to help you and your teams achieve strategic results.

www.leadershiphand.com

+1 703.820.8018 USA

Notes

[1] In a series of interviews I conducted with women. CEOs of technology businesses, I was struck by the unique way each defined growth. No matter how they defined growth, however, their strategies reflected the business stage they were in.

[2] Endeavor Global Inc. www.endeavor.org

[3] Teri-E Belf is the founder of the Success Unlimited Network®, and the first International Coach Federation Master Certified Coach. www.successunlimitednet.com

[4] *A Roadmap for Women's Economic Empowerment* was developed by the UN Foundation and the ExxonMobil Foundation. Its purpose is "to help identify the most effective interventions to empower women economically across four categories of employment – entrepreneurship, farming, wage employment and young women's employment." These "…must be targeted depending on particular economic and country contexts." www.womeneconroadmap.org

[5] Aspen Network of Development Entrepreneurs www.andeglobal.org

[6] International Finance Corporate www.ifc.org

[7] World Economic Forum www.weforum.org and www.weforum.org/issues/global-gender-gap

[8] Society for International Development www.sidw.org

[9] Please see Part 2 and the section on "An Alternate Universe." I believe Gneezy's and List's research explains why we have to make a continual effort.

[10] Vital Voices Global Partnership www.vitalvoices.org

[11] PBS *Makers Series* http://video.pbs.org/program/makers-women-who-make-america

[12] National Women's Business Council www.nwbc.gov

[13] Women's Foreign Policy Group www.wfpg.org

[14] For a timeline of women's suffrage:
http://en.wikipedia.org/wiki/Timeline_of_women%27s_suffrage

[15] Catalyst "Women CEOs of the S&P 500."
www.catalyst.org/knowledge/women-ceos-sp-500

[16] You can read more about this in Vazquez book: *Buying For Impact: How to Buy From Women and Change Our World.* Advantage Media Group (February 20, 2013) It is available on Amazon.com.

[17] WEConnect International helps women-owned businesses succeed in global value chains. It identifies, educates, registers, and certifies women's business enterprises based outside of the U.S., and then connects them with multinational corporate buyers. www.weconnectinternational.org

[18] Women's Business Enterprise National Council www.wbenc.org

[19] Faye Crosby's research cited in the *Harvard Business Review* https://hbr.org/2013/09/women-rising-the-unseen-barriers, *Harvard Business Review*, Herminia Ibarra, Robin Ely, Deborah Kolb, September, 2013. The study cited is "The Denial of Personal Discrimination" by Faye Crosby, *American Behavioral Scientist* Vol 27, No. 3. January/February, 1984, 371-386, @1984 Sage Publications, Inc. A special thank you to Provost Crosby, Cowell College at the University of California, Santa Cruz, for making this study available to me for *Hidden by Gender*. http://psychology.ucsc.edu

[20] This is from the Chris Argyris's body of seminal work on learning organizations.

[21] See the *Harvard Business Review* article: "Women Rising: The Unseen Barriers" by Herminia Ibarra, Robin J. Ely, Deborah Kolb, September, 2013. https://hbr.org/2013/09/women-rising-the-unseen-barriers

[22] See the *Harvard Business Review* article "How Female Leaders Should Handle Double-Standards" by Herminia Ibarra, February, 2013. https://hbr.org/2013/02/how-female-leaders-should-handle-double-standards/

[23] "Male Scientist Writes of Life as Female Scientist" by Shankar Vedantam, *Washington Post*, Thursday, July 13, 2006 www.washingtonpost.com/wp-dyn/content/article/2006/07/12/AR2006071201883.html

[24] iO Tillett Wright's *TEDxWomen* talk and transcript: http://www.ted.com/talks/io_tillett_wright_fifty_shades_of_gay?language=en

[25] *Spiritual Evolution: How We Are Wired for Faith, Hope, and Love Paperback* by George Vaillant, page 5. Harmony; Reprint edition (June 9, 2009)

[26] "Defend Your Research: What Makes a Team Smarter? More Women" by Anita Woolley and Thomas Malone *Harvard Business Review*, June, 2011 http://hbr.org/2011/06/defend-your-research-what-makes-a-team-smarter-more-women/ar/1

[27] In the original edition of *To Kill a Mockingbird* this quote is found on page 30.

[28] *Hidden in Plain Sight: Rapidly Discovering Solutions to Your Business & Leadership Issues* by Beth Hand, a Leadership Hand® Book, 2014. http://www.amazon.com/Hidden-Plain-Sight-Discovering-Leadership-ebook/dp/B00K6ME9MC

[29] The HeforShe Campaign is a solidarity campaign to engage men and boys as change agents for gender equality and women's rights, http://www.heforshe.org

[30] "The Role of Men and Boys in Achieving Gender Equality." United Nations, Division for the Advancement of Women, Department of Economic and Social Affairs, page 6, 2008.

[31] Ibid.

[32] Catalyst's "29 Actions Men Can Take to Create an Inclusive Workplace" http://www.catalyst.org/system/files/actions_men_can_take_to_create_an_inclusive_workplace.pdf

[33] You can find Ed Carr's work on "Gender and Climate Change Adaptation in Agrarian Settings" at his site. http://www.edwardrcarr.com

[34] A note of appreciation to Dr. Emerson Wickwire, an expert in sleep medicine and research in Baltimore, Maryland, who kindly helped me make this analysis simple and valid!

[35] Geert Hofstede www.geerthofstede.nl

[36] Geert Hofstede Dimensions http://www.geerthofstede.nl/dimensions-of-national-cultures

[37] Geert Hofstede Cultural Dimensions http://en.wikipedia.org/wiki/Hofstede%27s_cultural_dimensions_theory

[38] "Gender Differences In Competition: Evidence From A Matrilineal And A Patriarchal Society" by Uri Gneezy, Kenneth L. Leonard, John A. List. Working Paper 13727

http://www.nber.org/papers/w13727, National Bureau of Economic Research, January, 2008.

[39] "Where Women Are More Competitive Than Men" by Uri Gneezy and John List, *Time,* Nov. 04, 2013 http://ideas.time.com/2013/11/04/where-women-are-more-competitive-than-men/. Article adapted from the book *The Why Axis: Hidden Motives and the Undiscovered Economics of Everyday Life* by Uri Gneezy and John List. Excerpted by arrangement with PublicAffairs, a member of The Perseus Books Group. Copyright © 2013.

[40] Center for the Study of Neuroeconomics at George Mason University http://www.neuroeconomics.us

[41] For a fascinating example of a complex business transaction that turned into a diplomatic one, the story of Robert van Zwieten, now President and CEO of the Emerging Markets Private Equity Association, in *Hidden by Leadership Paradox: How to Navigate to Solutions in Between,* one of the books in the Leadership Hand® series.

[42] You can read more about Alex Cole in *Hidden by Leadership Paradox: How to Navigate to Solutions in Between.*

[43] U.S. champion heavy weight boxer Muhammed Ali created this catch phrase to describe his fighting style: Float like a butterfly, sting like a bee.

[44] International Finance Corporation http://www.ifc.org

[45] Enterprising Women Magazine https://enterprisingwomen.com

[46] Enterprising Women of Year Annual Awards Ceremony https://enterprisingwomen.com/annual-awards.html

[47] *Hidden in Plain Sight! Rapidly Discovering Solutions for Your Business & Leadership Issues*

[48] Creative Associates International
http://www.creativeassociatesinternational.com

[49] I first read about this concept in Michael Gerber's Book *The E-Myth Revisited.*

[50] Suzi Tucker is a gifted facilitator of family constellations, and teacher who works with groups and one-on-one. She has had a profound impact on my life. www.suzitucker.com

[51] United Nations Girl Up campaign unites girls to change the world. https://girlup.org

[52] Susan RoAne shared this wonderful phrase with me from her book titled *The Secrets of Savvy Networking: How to Make the Best Connections for Business and Personal Success.* Susan is personable, principled in what she advises, a professional speaker, and expert coach on publishing and how to work a room. www.SusanRoane.com

[53] The j. jane Project www.j-jane.com

[54] *Stand Out: How to Find Your Breakthrough Idea and Build a Following Around It* http://www.amazon.com/Stand-Out-Breakthrough-Following-Around/dp/1591847400/ref=la_B009FBO664_1_1?s=books&ie=UTF8&qid=1438095964&sr=1-1

[55] Giving Pledge http://givingpledge.org

[56] *Hidden by Assumptions: Seeing People & Solutions for Your Important Business Issues.*

[57] You can read more about CEO Harriet Lamb and Fairtrade's important work in the Leadership Hand® book *Hidden*

102

by Leadership Paradox: How to Navigate to Solutions in Between.
The Fairtrade International site is www.fairtrade.net

[58] *A Small Section of the World*
http://asmallsectionoftheworld.com

[59] *Bossypants* by Tina Fey, Little Brown and Company,
Hachette Book Group. NY, NY 2011, pages 143-145

[60] Laurel Bartlett, Dragonfly Communication
http://dragonflycommunication.com

[61] Joanne Lozar Glenn http://joannelozarglenn.com

[62] Sara Martinez. Email: sarahtinez7@gmail.com

[63] Kholoud H. Email: kholoudyoussef@gmail.com

Made in the USA
Middletown, DE
30 September 2016